maple syrup
40 TRIED & TRUE RECIPES

Corrine Kozlak
photography by Kevin Scott Ramos

Adventure Publications
Cambridge, Minnesota

Cover and book design by Lora Westberg
Edited by Emily Beaumont

Cover images: All images by Kevin Scott Ramos
All images copyrighted.

All images by Kevin Scott Ramos unless otherwise noted.
Corrine Kozlak: 17 top right, bottom; 22
Used under license from Shutterstock.com:
Guy Banville: 16 top; Sylvie Bouchard: 19; Cindy Creighton: 18;
ffolas: 24; Fotofermer: 14; iyd39: 20-21; Kim D. Lyman: 23 bottom;
Tim Masters: 17 top left; **T.M. McCarthy:** 15; Pinkcandy: 16 bottom;
showcake: 11; sianc: 23 top; Sweet Memento Photography: 4-5

10 9 8 7 6 5 4 3

Maple Syrup: 40 Tried & True Recipes
Copyright © 2020 by Corrine Kozlak
Published by Adventure Publications
An imprint of AdventureKEEN
310 Garfield Street South
Cambridge, Minnesota 55008
(800) 678-7006
www.adventurepublications.net
Printed in China
ISBN 978-1-59193-931-3 (pbk.); ISBN 978-1-59193-932-0 (ebook)

maple syrup

40 TRIED & TRUE RECIPES

Acknowledgments

I would like to express my gratitude to all who contributed and helped me create this cookbook, especially the following:

- The photographer Kevin Ramos, who gave freely of his time and talent— way beyond his compensation

- Kim McElheny, for her skillful post-production photo work, her enthusiasm, artful eye, and fabulous organizational skills

- My family: Dan, Danny, and Callie Kozlak, for tasting recipes and helping me with my computer and writing questions, and Erin, my daughter-in-law, who inspired the gluten-free additions

- My mom and dad, for gathering personal, handwritten recipes, as well as newspaper-clipped ones; letting me borrow favorite cookbooks; and providing many of the props used in the photos

- My Canadian sister-in-law, Cheri, who shared her favorite maple syrup recipes and cookbook authors and was so helpful when I was first developing the cookbook

- My cousin Julie, and her daughter, Ceci, who put up with my many attempts to get the maple fudge and oatmeal recipes just right

- My dear niece Tiana; her husband, Eric; and baby Aurora for hosting us at their Sunset Resort on Houghton Lake, in Michigan, for our sugar shack weekend

- "My girls" and especially Vicki, for the generous sharing of her personal recipes

- Frank and Tina Ziegler, without whose support, love, and professional advice I would not have gotten this project going

- And a great many thanks to all of my family and friends, who were very supportive during this project and who freely answered the question, "What is your favorite way to use maple syrup?"

maple syrup

40 TRIED & TRUE RECIPES

Table of Contents

Preface

I have always loved maple syrup. When I was a child, my family had pancakes every Saturday morning. We mostly enjoyed the Bisquick type served with Aunt Jemima syrup, but sometimes my father would make buckwheat pancakes and serve them with real maple syrup. This was prior to the rise of the natural food movement; looking back, he was years ahead of his time with his fancy breakfasts!

This cookbook is the culmination of all of my maple syrup discoveries since those early days. Over the past several years, I've immersed myself in collecting, testing, and tasting many maple syrup recipes. The 40 tried-and-true ones in this book have been approved by friends and family, then carefully edited and professionally photographed.

In my work on this book, I've also collected sugar maple leaves and studied the long history of maple syrup from its presence as a historic staple of Native Americans to its myriad of uses today.

I also got a hands-on look at the process of making maple syrup when I visited a few sugar shacks in northern Michigan. This gave me a whole new appreciation for hardworking maple farmers and their families, who collect each year's tree sap in a short window of time and then turn it into syrup. While the basic process of making maple syrup is simple (see page 22 to try it yourself), producing it in bulk is complicated, as it requires specialized equipment and is very time- and temperature-sensitive.

Of course, you know it's wonderful on pancakes and waffles, and I've included those recipes, but maple syrup is an incredibly versatile ingredient. You will be surprised and delighted at what just a little bit of maple syrup will do for Brussels sprouts, sweet potatoes, salmon, or cookies. And if you thought bacon couldn't get any better, just try it maple-glazed.

Tree to Table

Maple syrup is a wonderful gift from nature. As its name suggests, it's produced from the sap of maple trees. Maple trees belong to the genus *Acer*; several different maple species can produce the sap needed to make maple syrup, but the sap from the Sugar Maple (*Acer saccharum*) tree has the highest sugar content. (Other trees, including birch, also possess sap that can be used to create a syrup-like product.) Once collected, the sap is boiled, and the excess water is turned to steam, leaving maple syrup behind.

Maple trees exist naturally in much of the eastern half of North America, but more than 70% of the world's supply of maple syrup is produced in eastern Canada, especially in the provinces of Quebec and Ontario. In the United States, Vermont produces the most syrup, followed by New York and Maine. States as far west as Minnesota also produce maple syrup, but not nearly as much.

On average, about 40 gallons of sap are required to produce 1 gallon of maple syrup. A maple tree is often 40 years old and at least 12 inches in diameter before it is tapped, and the average tree produces 10 gallons of sap, enough for about 1 quart (4 cups) of syrup.

Maple Syrup History

Long before European settlers arrived, Native Americans were the first to discover the sweet sap of the maple tree. While there are no records that mention maple products being present at the first Thanksgiving, which has been romanticized far beyond what we know actually occurred from the historical record, I like to think that maple products could have been served at the three-day feast between the Pilgrims and the Wampanoag Indians in 1621. If so, imagine what a treat the new sweet taste might have been.

Maple syrup's origins date back centuries, and a few folktales tell the story of its discovery. In one account often attributed to the Abenaki Indians, maple syrup once flowed from the trees like honey. The Creator became concerned that having maple syrup so easily available might make the people complacent. So the Creator told a man named Gluskabe to pour water into the trees. This diluted the sap, making it run only for a short time, making maple syrup much more difficult to produce.

In an Iroquois telling, the first syrup-maker was an Iroquois woman, the wife of one Chief Wokis. One evening in late winter the chief embedded his tomahawk in a maple tree. The next morning when he left for a hunt, he pulled the tomahawk out and the sap happened to drain into a birch-bark container. The sap was discovered by his wife and she used it to cook meat all day. When he came home he was very pleased with the taste of the sweetened meat.

Maple syrup even made appearances in the political history of the U.S.; during the Revolutionary War, it was deemed a more "moral" sugar (instead of slave-produced sugar cane). A similar argument was made in the Civil War in the North, favoring maple sugar over molasses and sugar produced by slaves.

How Maple Syrup Is Made

Maple sap begins to flow in late winter and early spring (usually in February and March), but the exact timing depends on local weather conditions. Sap begins to flow when alternating freezing and thawing cycles lead to a buildup of pressure that forces the sap out of the tree. Maple season lasts only 6 to 10 weeks, and sap runs heavily for only 10 to 20 of those days. If the weather doesn't cooperate (excessive heat and cold can both be problems), sap production falters. In addition, once the trees begin to bud, the composition of the sap changes and it loses its trademark taste, becoming unpalatable. When that happens, the season's over.

The simplest way to make maple syrup is also among the oldest: one simply drills a hole in an appropriately sized tree (see page 22), adds a tap, and then affixes a bucket beneath it to collect the sap.

When it's collected, maple sap is a colorless, slightly sweet liquid; it stays viable in this form for only a matter of days, requiring temperatures of 38 degrees or colder to prevent bacterial growth. Time is of the essence when maple syruping.

In the old days, galvanized buckets full of sap were emptied by hand, and then brought via horse and cart directly to a sugar shack, the building where sap is boiled down into syrup.

Today, modern technology makes sap collection faster than ever. Power tools can make tapping trees easier. Plastic tubing runs from tree to tree, and a special machine that creates a slight vacuum moves sap into a central collection container. From here, the sap goes through a reverse-osmosis machine that concentrates the sugars and then transfers them into an evaporator pan. The combined process requires a lot of energy; electrical power for the vacuum system is provided by a battery or a standard electrical connection, and the heat for boiling the syrup is provided by wood or gas. The evaporator needs to be constantly monitored until the sap reaches 219 degrees. The resulting syrup is then filtered, cooled, and sanitarily bottled or barreled. When properly handled, maple syrup has a long shelf life.

Maple Syrup Grading

Both in the U.S. and Canada, maple syrup is carefully regulated and commercial maple syrup makers are licensed, though the specific licensing rules vary from state to state.

Maple syrup is also carefully graded based on color, flavor, and appearance. As a general rule, darker syrups have a stronger taste. According to the USDA, there are four primary consumer grades of maple syrup:

- U.S. Grade A Golden (delicate taste)
- U.S. Grade A Amber (rich taste)
- U.S. Grade A Dark (robust taste)
- U.S. Grade A Very Dark (strong taste)

There's also a Grade B variety, which is not sold to consumers, but is used to make other products.

All the recipes in this book were made and tested with Grade A Pure Maple Syrup, but you can vary the syrup you use depending on your taste. One thing to avoid, however, is using maple-flavored table syrup, which is often not maple syrup at all but produced with corn syrup and the like.

Sugar Shack Fun

Maple sap is the first crop of spring, and to winter-weary folks in the Upper Midwest and the Northeast, this ritual is a sure sign that spring is on its way. And what better month than March to do something fun and interesting. There is something nostalgic and beautiful about galvanized buckets hanging from maple trees, knowing that pure maple syrup is on its way.

Every year in early spring all over the Upper Midwest and the Northeastern United States and Canada, people celebrate maple syrup with festivals and sugar shack open houses. Maple syrup producers welcome visitors to their sugar shacks to watch how nature's gift of sweet watery sap becomes the maple syrup we all love. Tours, demonstrations, and samplings of the product are part of the fun, but tours are often limited to one or two days a year, so plan ahead if visiting a sugar shack is on your (galvanized) bucket list.

I recently visited sugar shacks in northern Michigan. It was so interesting to see the process in action, and after our tour we were given the delicious treat of maple syrup over vanilla ice cream. This is an absolutely delightful combination and one that I heartily recommend. Maple syrup may also be used as a sweetener in coffee.

Sugar on Snow

Sugar on Snow (sometimes called "leather aprons") is a traditional, fun way to taste freshly created syrup. One maple syrup farmer told me that her grandchildren call it "Grandma candy." Sugar on Snow is created by pouring hot (234 degrees) maple syrup in a thin coating of strips onto well–packed snow or shaved ice. The syrup turns taffy-like but is too soft to pick up. It is then wound onto forks, and kids and adults alike love this sweet, natural treat. In Maine it is often served with sour pickles and plain doughnuts to contrast with the sweet flavor.

Do-It-Yourself Maple Syruping or Backyard Sugaring

If you have access to mature maple trees (they need to be at least 12 inches in diameter, or else you may damage the tree), you can partake in the spring ritual of collecting sap and making your own maple syrup. Known as "sugar bushes," the seven most common syrup-producing trees are: Sugar Maple, Black Maple, Red Maple, Silver Maple, Boxelder, Norway Maple, and Bigleaf Maple. Sugar Maple and Black Maple produce the most sap and the ideal syrup we all love. Start by identifying tappable trees in the fall. Tie a string around the prospective trees or somehow mark them. (You'll find that leafless trees in March can look a lot alike.)

Equipment

- Power drill and a ⁵/₁₆" drill bit
- Spiles or tapping spouts
- Hammer
- Covered collection containers
- Large, shallow boiling pan or kettle
- Heat source (campfire, grill, or camp stove)
- Candy thermometer
- Filter material (cheesecloth or felt)
- Glass bottles with caps

When to Tap Trees

Timing is everything when it comes to maple syrup. The season occurs in very early spring, with sap beginning to flow when there are freezing temperatures at night, but balmier weather (often into the 40s) during the day. The timing of syruping season can vary by a matter of weeks from year to year, but the season typically happens in March. And sometimes, seasons end early. If temperatures stay above freezing and the trees begin to bud, the season is over. Sap collected after budding begins is dark and bitter.

How to Tap Trees

First, start by drilling a hole approximately 2–4 feet above the ground. When drilling, angle the bit upward a little, and drill about 3 inches into the tree. Then, gently hammer in the spile (the tap), and hang your container from the spile. Empty the containers each day into food-grade sterile containers; if it's warm, do so more than once a day.

It takes about 40 gallons of sap to create 1 gallon of maple syrup; on average, each tree provides approximately 10–20 gallons of sap. Refrigerate the sap (38 degrees or cooler) to prevent it from spoiling. You'll usually want to collect 10 gallons of sap before starting the boil-down; this amount should yield about 1 quart of syrup.

From Sap to Syrup

Maple sap must be boiled, and the excess water content evaporated, before it becomes maple syrup. Backyard maple producers use the batch system. Start the process outside in a large pan/pot using wood or gas as fuel. As the water evaporates, add more maple sap, but make sure it keeps boiling. Repeat this process, and use a candy thermometer to monitor the temperature. Eventually, the sap will start to look darker, and its bubbles will shrink; at that point, transfer the sap to a smaller pot, and boil it indoors until it reaches 219 degrees. Keep a watchful eye on it and don't let it boil over. Once it reaches 219 degrees, it's turned into syrup! While still hot, strain the syrup through cheesecloth or a felt filter, pour into sterilized jars, and store in a cool dry place. Refrigerate it after opening.

Cleaning Up

Don't use detergents; instead, clean all equipment with 1 part bleach to 20 parts hot water and double rinse. Store equipment in a dry place and keep it covered; do not use buckets and containers for any nonfood purposes.

Cooking and Baking with Maple Syrup

All the recipes in this book were made and tested with Grade A Pure Maple Syrup (see page 18).

If you want to substitute maple syrup into a recipe that calls for sugar, you can! Generally speaking, when substituting maple syrup for sugar, you need to reduce the liquid in the recipe by 3 tablespoons for every 1 cup of maple syrup used.

Here are some handy equivalents:

- 1 cup of sugar = ¾ cup maple syrup
- 1 cup honey = ¾ cup maple syrup + ½ cup sugar
- Maple syrup can be substituted for molasses on a 1:1 basis.

Note: Because maple syrup is a liquid, when you're substituting, watch for changes in consistency and compensate as needed. Also note that the color of your baked products will vary.

Maple Syrup Cooking Tips

The best way to heat maple syrup or melt butter is to do so in a glass measuring cup (such as Pyrex) in the microwave.

Maple syrup heats up very quickly. Start by heating for 30 seconds; test and go from there.

When measuring maple syrup, scrape the sides of your measuring cup well, as it has a tendency to coat and you may lose a fair amount in the process.

Some baking recipes direct you to "make a well" in the center of a flour mixture. This means you are to create an indentation, which pushes the flour mixture up onto the sides of the bowl.

When butter is called for, it is always unsalted.

I call for the use of a food processor in quite a few of the recipes. I find this is the best tool for emulsification, fine chopping, and working fat into flour.

Caramelization occurs when the sugar in food is heated, developing a sweet nutty flavor and a brown color.

Mise en place is a French phrase meaning "everything in its place." I find that collecting all of my ingredients, equipment, and sometimes measuring everything out before cooking or baking makes for a more accurate and stress-free cooking experience.

When eggs are called for, it means large eggs.

Double boiler: If you do not own a pan that is specifically designed as a double boiler, you can easily fashion one yourself with a medium-size pot and a heatproof bowl. To do so, fill the pot about ¼ full with water and bring it to a simmer. Fit the bowl into the pot. The bottom of the bowl should not reach the water. Add ingredients into the bowl, and proceed with the recipe. (You may require heat protection for your hands when handling the bowl with this method.)

breads and breakfast

Best Basic Buttermilk Pancakes

This recipe makes fluffy, mottled pancakes with crisp edges.
If you want solid-colored pancakes, use little to no fat on the griddle.

makes 12–16 pancakes

INGREDIENTS
2 cups all-purpose flour*
2 tablespoons sugar
2 teaspoons baking powder
½ teaspoon baking soda
½ teaspoon kosher salt
2 cups buttermilk
2 large eggs
2 tablespoons butter, melted
    and cooled
1 tablespoon lemon juice
Vegetable oil

TOPPINGS
softened butter, warm maple
    syrup, fresh fruit

In a large bowl, whisk together flour, sugar, baking powder, baking soda, and salt; make a well in center of mixture.

In a large glass measuring cup, whisk buttermilk, eggs, 2 tablespoons melted butter, and lemon juice to combine. Pour buttermilk mixture into well of flour mixture; gently combine. (A few lumps are desired.) Let batter rest 10 minutes.

Heat griddle to 375° or a nonstick pan to medium-high heat. Add a thin layer of oil and butter to the hot surface. Pour ¼ cup batter onto griddle for each pancake; cook until top is bubbly and edges are slightly dry, about 2 to 3 minutes on each side. Serve hot with desired toppings.

* Gluten-free flour may be substituted.

Oatmeal B&B Pancakes

This recipe was given to me by my dad, the chief pancake maker in our house, where pancakes were a Saturday morning ritual. He first tasted them at a bed-and-breakfast in Vancouver, Canada, where he asked for the recipe. This is my slightly adapted version.

makes 12 pancakes

INGREDIENTS

1 cup old-fashioned oats
1 cup whole-wheat flour
2 tablespoons sugar
1 teaspoon baking soda
1 teaspoon baking powder
1 teaspoon salt
3 tablespoons butter, chilled
2 cups buttermilk
2 eggs
2 teaspoons vanilla extract
Vegetable oil
3 cups blueberries, divided
1 cup maple syrup

In the bowl of a food processor with a metal blade, process oats 45 seconds. Add flour, sugar, baking soda, baking powder, and salt; pulse to combine. Sprinkle cold butter pieces on top, and process until mixture forms coarse crumbs. Transfer to a large bowl; make a well in center of mixture.

In a large glass measuring cup, whisk buttermilk, eggs, and vanilla to combine. Pour buttermilk mixture into well of flour mixture and gently combine. (A few lumps are desired.)

Brush a large nonstick griddle or skillet with oil; bring to medium-high heat. Pour ¼ cup batter onto griddle for each pancake; cook until top is bubbly and edges are slightly dry, about 2 to 3 minutes on each side.

Meanwhile, cook 1½ cups blueberries with maple syrup in a small saucepan over medium heat for 2 minutes. Mash cooked blueberries and strain syrup. Stir in remaining 1½ cups whole blueberries. Serve warm over pancakes.

Best Basic Waffles

This is my favorite basic waffle recipe because it works well every time—
and I've tried it in three different waffle irons! This will appeal to those who like a crisper waffle.

makes 6 waffles

INGREDIENTS

2 cups all-purpose flour
4 tablespoons sugar, divided
4 teaspoons baking powder
½ teaspoon salt
1½ cups milk
2 eggs
⅓ cup butter, melted and cooled
1 teaspoon vanilla extract
3 cups strawberries, hulled
   and quartered

TOPPINGS

softened butter, warmed
   maple syrup

In a large bowl, whisk together flour, 2 tablespoons sugar, baking powder, and salt; make a well in center of mixture.

In a large glass measuring cup, whisk together milk, eggs, butter, and vanilla to combine.

Pour milk mixture into well of flour mixture and gently combine. Let batter rest 10 minutes.

Meanwhile, in a medium bowl, toss strawberries with remaining 2 tablespoons sugar. Let stand at least 20 minutes or until strawberries become syrupy.

Heat a lightly greased waffle iron and cook according to manufacturer's instructions. (It usually takes about ½ cup batter per waffle.) Keep waffles crisp in a low-temperature oven until ready to serve. If necessary, reheat waffles on buttered waffle iron for 30 seconds. Serve with strawberries and desired toppings.

Pumpkin Waffles

· ·

Pumpkin is not just for Thanksgiving! Pumpkin and maple syrup come together beautifully in this recipe for waffles. Your kitchen will smell wonderful while these are cooking!

· ·

makes 6 waffles

INGREDIENTS
2 cups all-purpose flour
⅓ cup sugar
2 teaspoons baking powder
½ teaspoon cinnamon
¼ teaspoon ground ginger
⅛ teaspoon fresh nutmeg
½ teaspoon salt
6 tablespoons unsalted butter,
  cubed and chilled
½ cup whole milk
½ cup heavy cream
⅓ cup pumpkin puree
3 eggs
1 teaspoon vanilla or
  maple extract

TOPPINGS
sour cream, softened butter,
  warm maple syrup, pepitas

In the bowl of a food processor with a metal blade, pulse flour, sugar, baking powder, cinnamon, ginger, nutmeg, and salt to combine. Sprinkle cold butter pieces on top, and process until mixture forms coarse crumbs. Transfer to a large bowl; make a well in center of mixture.

In a large glass measuring cup, whisk milk, cream, pumpkin, eggs, and vanilla to combine. Pour milk mixture into well of flour mixture and gently combine. (A few lumps are desired.)

Heat a lightly greased waffle iron and cook according to manufacturer's instructions. (It usually takes about ½ cup batter per waffle.) Keep waffles crisp in a low-temperature oven until ready to serve. If necessary, reheat waffles on buttered waffle iron for 30 seconds. Serve waffles hot with desired toppings.

Maple Syrup–Glazed Bacon

This sweet-salt-fat combination takes beloved bacon to
greater heights. The neat and tasty technique makes bacon a stand-alone
buffet item or a fun garnish for a Bloody Mary (page 110).

makes 12 pieces

INGREDIENTS
1 pound thick-sliced bacon
3 tablespoons maple syrup

Heat oven to 350°. Line a heavy rimmed half-sheet pan or jelly roll pan with aluminum foil.

Spread bacon flat on prepared pan. Bake 20 minutes. Remove cooked bacon to paper towels; discard bacon grease from baking sheet. Place an oven-safe cooling rack on baking pan. Place cooked bacon on rack. and brush one side lightly with maple syrup. Bake 10 minutes or until syrup has caramelized and bacon is cooked to desired crispness.

Maple-Vanilla Granola

· ·

This delicious, cost-effective, gluten-free granola may be stored
in an airtight container at room temperature up to 3 weeks.
Layer it with yogurt for an on-the-go breakfast.

· ·

makes 9 cups

INGREDIENTS
½ cup maple syrup
½ cup coconut oil, melted
2 teaspoons vanilla extract
3 cups old-fashioned rolled oats*
1 cup sliced almonds
1 cup pepitas
1 cup sunflower seeds
1 cup pistachios
⅓ cup ground flaxseed
½ teaspoon salt
⅛ teaspoon cinnamon
1 cup dried cherries

Preheat oven to 300°. Line 2 rimmed baking sheets with
parchment paper.

In a large measuring cup, whisk together maple syrup,
coconut oil, and vanilla.

Toss together oats, almonds, pepitas, sunflower seeds,
pistachios, flaxseed, salt, and cinnamon in a large bowl.
Pour maple mixture over oats mixture; stir until
completely coated.

Spread onto prepared baking sheets and bake 40 to 50
minutes, stirring every 20 minutes, until lightly browned.
Stir in cherries. Cool completely before serving.

*Oats are naturally gluten-free but are often processed in
facilities with wheat. Gluten-free oats are available; check
the packaging to be sure.

Best Maple Banana Bread

This moist banana bread started as a recipe submitted to the *Chicago Tribune*.
It has evolved over the years, and I have added a delicious maple glaze to make it even better.
This is a great use for those overripe bananas that many of us keep in our freezers!

makes 6 mini-loaves or 2 (9x5-inch) loaves

BREAD
3½ cups plus 1 tablespoon
    all-purpose flour, divided
2 teaspoons baking soda
2 teaspoons baking powder
1 teaspoon ground cinnamon
2 cups chopped walnuts
    or pecans
2 cups light brown sugar,
    firmly packed
4 large eggs
1¼ cups canola oil
1 (8-ounce) container sour cream
1 tablespoon maple extract
3 cups (about 8 large) very ripe
    bananas, mashed with a fork

GLAZE
¼ cup butter
½ cup maple syrup
½ teaspoon maple extract
1 cup powdered sugar, sifted

Preheat oven to 350°. Lightly grease 2 (9x5-inch) loaf pans or 6 mini-loaf pans; line with parchment or wax paper.

To make bread, whisk together 3½ cups flour, baking soda, baking powder, and cinnamon in a large bowl. In a medium bowl, toss nuts in remaining 1 tablespoon flour.

Place brown sugar in the bowl of a stand-up electric mixer; add eggs, one at a time, mixing on slow speed until combined. With mixer running, add oil. Add sour cream and 1 tablespoon maple extract, mixing until combined.

Add half flour mixture to brown sugar mixture; stir in mashed bananas. Stir in remaining half flour mixture and flour-coated nuts. Pour batter into prepared pans, filling ¾ full; smooth tops.

Bake 70 to 80 minutes (less for small pans) until bread rises and a toothpick inserted in center comes out clean. Cool.

To make glaze, melt butter in a small pan over medium heat; stir in maple syrup. Stir while boiling for 2 minutes. Remove from heat; stir in ½ teaspoon maple extract. Add powdered sugar; whisk until smooth. Stir 3 to 5 minutes or until mixture begins to thicken and cool slightly. Drizzle over bread.

Maple-Frosted Pumpkin Muffins

Pumpkin and maple marry well. Every year, the flavor of pumpkin signals the beginning of fall.

makes 10 muffins

MUFFINS
1 cup whole-wheat flour
¾ cup unbleached
   all-purpose flour
1 teaspoon baking soda
½ teaspoon baking powder
½ teaspoon cloves
½ teaspoon cinnamon
½ teaspoon nutmeg
¼ teaspoon salt
6 tablespoons granulated sugar
1 cup pumpkin puree
¼ cup vegetable oil
¼ cup maple syrup
1½ tablespoons milk
2 eggs

GLAZE
3 tablespoons butter
⅓ cup maple syrup
¼ teaspoon maple extract
¾ cup powdered sugar

GARNISH
pumpkin seeds

Preheat oven to 350°. Lightly grease muffin pans.

To make muffins, sift together whole-wheat flour and next 8 ingredients in a large bowl. Make a well in center of mixture. In a large glass measuring cup, beat together pumpkin, oil, ¼ cup maple syrup, milk, and eggs. Pour pumpkin mixture into well of flour mixture and gently combine. Scoop batter into prepared muffin cups, filling ¾ full. Bake 20 minutes or until a toothpick inserted in center comes out clean. Cool.

To make glaze, melt butter over medium heat in a medium saucepan; whisk in ⅓ cup maple syrup. Bring to a boil, and cook, stirring constantly, 2 minutes. Remove from heat and stir in maple extract. Sift in powdered sugar, and whisk until smooth and slightly thick; drizzle onto muffins. Garnish, if desired.

Overnight Oatmeal

Do you have winter overnight guests? Make this big batch of oatmeal in the liner of a slow cooker the night before, and refrigerate. Heat it up in the slow cooker the next morning, and put out bowls of toppings for an oatmeal bar.

makes 6 servings

INGREDIENTS
4 cups milk or oat milk
¾ cup maple syrup
½ teaspoon cinnamon
¼ teaspoon salt
2 cups old-fashioned oats

TOPPINGS
maple syrup, applesauce, peanut butter, chopped nuts, fresh berries, sliced bananas, honey, brown sugar, and cinnamon sugar

Lightly grease the liner of a 4- to 6-quart slow cooker.

Whisk together milk, syrup, cinnamon, and salt in a large bowl; stir in oats. Transfer mixture to liner. Refrigerate overnight.

Heat oatmeal in slow cooker on medium-high heat, stirring occasionally until warm.

Add more milk if oatmeal is too thick.

Serve with desired toppings and additional milk.

Monte Cristo Breakfast Sandwiches

These meat-and-cheese French toast sandwiches are classic, with the perfect combination of breakfast flavors.

makes 4 servings

INGREDIENTS

4 slices maple-flavored bacon
¾ cup maple syrup
2 eggs
¼ cup milk
2 tablespoons Dijon mustard
½ teaspoon paprika
1 dash cayenne pepper
8 slices firm country-style
   white bread
8 slices (4 ounces)
   Gruyère cheese
8 slices (8 ounces)
   deli-sliced ham
4 slices (4 ounces)
   deli-sliced turkey
2 tablespoons butter

Cook bacon in a skillet over medium heat until crispy. Remove and drain on paper towels; chop. Pour maple syrup into a small saucepan; stir in bacon and keep warm.

In a shallow flat-bottomed dish, lightly beat eggs, milk, mustard, paprika, and cayenne until combined; set aside.

Top each of 4 slices of bread in this order: 1 slice cheese, 1 slice ham, 1 slice turkey, 1 slice ham, and 1 slice cheese; top each with a remaining slice of bread. Press down on sandwiches slightly.

Melt butter in a frying pan or Panini grill over medium heat. Dip both sides of sandwiches in egg mixture. When butter in pan is hot, fry sandwiches until golden brown, about 3 to 4 minutes on each side. Serve with warm maple-bacon syrup.

Fried Chicken and Waffles

· ·

This combination became popular in its current form as a meal served in the Harlem restaurant Wells Supper Club. Leftover fried chicken was paired with waffles and maple syrup and served to very late-night/early-morning customers. I use boneless chicken here; however, bone-in dark meat is traditionally preferred.

· ·

makes 4 servings

INGREDIENTS
3 cups low-fat buttermilk, divided
2 large eggs
1 stick butter, melted and cooled
3 cups unbleached all-purpose flour
2½ teaspoons baking powder
½ teaspoon baking soda
¾ teaspoon salt
4 boneless chicken cutlets (1 pound)
Salt and freshly ground black pepper, to taste
1 cup vegetable oil

TOPPINGS
butter, maple syrup, hot sauce

Whisk together 2 cups buttermilk, eggs, and butter in a large glass measuring cup. In a large bowl, whisk together flour, baking powder, baking soda, and ¾ teaspoon salt. Place 1 cup flour mixture in a shallow dish; pour remaining 1 cup of buttermilk into a separate shallow dish. Set dishes aside.

Make a well in center of remaining flour mixture. Pour buttermilk mixture into well and gently combine. Set batter aside.

Season chicken on both sides with salt and pepper. Dredge cutlets in reserved flour mixture in shallow dish. Shake off excess. Dip chicken in buttermilk in shallow dish, then again in flour mixture. Place coated chicken on a cooling rack to dry slightly.

To make waffles, heat a lightly greased waffle iron and cook waffle batter according to manufacturer's instructions. Keep waffles crisp in a low-temperature oven until ready to serve. If necessary, reheat waffles on buttered waffle iron for 30 seconds.

To make fried chicken, heat oil in a large skillet over medium-high heat. Cook chicken in batches, 1 to 2 minutes per side, until golden brown and internal temperature reaches 175°. Transfer to a plate lined with paper towels.

Serve chicken on waffles with desired toppings.

Baked French Toast

Prepared the night before, this French toast is an indulgent and delicious breakfast or brunch dish.

makes 8–10 servings

INGREDIENTS

10 cups challah (egg twist bread), cut into ¾-inch cubes
¾ cup butter, melted
1 cup blueberries
1 cup sliced strawberries
1 (8-ounce) package cream cheese, cut into 30 cubes
1 cup whole milk
1 cup half-and-half
6 eggs
1 teaspoon vanilla extract
¼ teaspoon salt
¼ cup brown sugar
¼ teaspoon cinnamon
¼ cup maple syrup

TOPPING

warm maple syrup

Lightly toast bread cubes in oven, if needed. Spread melted butter into bottom of a 9x13-inch baking pan.* Arrange half of bread cubes to cover bottom of pan. Sprinkle fruit and cream cheese cubes evenly over bread. Top with remaining half of bread cubes.

Pour milk and half-and-half into a large bowl; whisk in eggs, vanilla, and salt. Pour milk mixture over bread, flipping bread pieces to coat, if necessary.

Combine brown sugar and cinnamon; sprinkle over bread mixture, and then drizzle with ¼ cup maple syrup. Tightly cover pan with plastic wrap, and refrigerate overnight.

Preheat oven to 350°. Meanwhile, bring pan to room temperature. Bake, uncovered, 25 to 30 minutes or until puffy and golden. Serve with warm maple syrup.

*This recipe can also be made in 10 (1-cup) individual soufflé dishes.

Maple Monkey Bread

• •

This is a five-ingredient, indulgent brunch treat that everyone loves.
When I recently served this at a bed-and-breakfast, a cheer
rang out as I presented the buttery sweet dome to the table.
The guests easily helped themselves to this maple-flavored treat.

• •

makes 12 servings

INGREDIENTS

½ cup maple sugar or
    granulated sugar
1 teaspoon cinnamon
¾ cup butter
2 (16-ounce) cans butter-
    flavored refrigerated biscuits
½ cup maple syrup

Preheat oven to 350°. Lightly grease a Bundt pan.

In a shallow bowl, combine sugar and cinnamon. In a large
glass measuring cup, microwave butter 30 to 60 seconds on
high or until melted.

Cut each biscuit into quarters. Dip biscuit quarters first in
melted butter and then in sugar mixture. Distribute evenly in
prepared pan. Stir maple syrup into remaining melted butter,
and pour entire mixture over biscuit quarters in pan.

Bake 25 minutes or until golden brown and center is cooked
through. (Do not overbake.)

Remove from oven, and let sit 10 minutes. Place a plate or
a rimmed pedestal on Bundt pan; protect your hands from
heat, and flip bread over onto plate. The syrup will run out
around the base. Serve immediately.

entrées

Maple-Soy Glazed Salmon

. . . .

This is delicious topped with a lightly cooked mixture of tomato, onion, and garlic.
Asparagus or broccoli makes for a healthy accompaniment.

. . . .

makes 2–4 servings

INGREDIENTS
¼ cup soy sauce*
2 tablespoons maple syrup
2 tablespoons cilantro, chopped
2 tablespoons sweet chili sauce*
2–4 (6-ounce) salmon fillets

Preheat oven to 375°. Line a baking sheet with parchment paper.

Combine soy sauce, maple syrup, cilantro, and chili sauce in a shallow glass dish. Marinate salmon in glaze 5 minutes on each side.

Place salmon on prepared pan, and bake 12 minutes.

*Gluten-free versions may be substituted.

Maple Rub Pulled Pork

The "low and slow" cooking of a pork shoulder rewards you with 7 pounds of great sandwich meat. This recipe pairs nicely with the Maple Baked Beans on page 76. Add your favorite maple-flavored barbecue sauce, soft buns, and coleslaw for a crowd-pleasing meal.

makes 12–14 servings

INGREDIENTS
¼ cup maple sugar
¼ cup kosher salt
3 tablespoons paprika
1½ tablespoons garlic powder
1½ tablespoons onion powder
1½ tablespoons black pepper
1 (8- to 9-pound) bone-in
   pork shoulder
2 cups water
Hamburger buns

TOPPINGS
purchased maple-flavored
   barbecue sauce, coleslaw

To make rub, combine maple sugar and next 5 ingredients in a small bowl. Coat roast all over with rub. Roast can be refrigerated, uncovered, overnight.

Preheat oven to 250°.

Pour 2 cups water in a large roasting pan with rack. Place roast, fat side up, on rack in pan. Bake 10 to 11 hours or until a thermometer registers 170°. (Check several areas of the roast.)

Transfer roast to a cutting board; let rest 20 minutes. Thinly slice or pull pork pieces off, discarding any fat. Serve on buns with desired toppings.

Maple–Brined Pork Chops

Sometimes all you want is a good pork chop. This brine gives great flavor as it tenderizes and keeps the chops moist. Allow for 4 hours of brining time.

makes 4 servings

INGREDIENTS
2¼ cups water
½ cup white vinegar
5½ tablespoons maple syrup, divided
3 tablespoons salt
1 teaspoon whole peppercorns
2 bay leaves
2 cloves garlic
Four bone-in pork chops
Salt and pepper, to taste
3 tablespoons butter

In a medium pot over medium heat, combine 2¼ cups water, vinegar, 4 tablespoons maple syrup, salt, peppercorns, bay leaves, and garlic; simmer 3 minutes. Transfer brine to a shallow dish, and let cool. Marinate pork chops in cooled brine in refrigerator for at least 4 hours.

Remove pork chops from brine; discard liquid and pat chops dry. Season both sides with salt and pepper. Sear pork chops in a cast iron or oven-safe pan 2 minutes on each side (or grill 2 minutes on each side).

Preheat oven to 300º.

In a glass measuring cup, microwave butter and remaining 1½ tablespoons maple syrup 30 seconds or until butter is melted. Pour butter mixture into pan, turning to coat chops.

Transfer pan to oven and bake 10 minutes or until internal temperature reaches 145º. Allow chops to rest 3 minutes before serving.

Maple-Teriyaki Marinade

This marinade helps to tenderize meat, while giving it a sweet-salty onion flavor.
It works nicely with skirt steak as well.

makes 1¼ cups

INGREDIENTS
1 tablespoon garlic
1 tablespoon fresh ginger
2 tablespoons minced shallots
½ cup tamari/soy sauce
½ cup maple syrup
2 tablespoons canola oil
2 tablespoons sesame seeds
1½ pounds flank steak

In the bowl of a food processor with a metal blade, process garlic, ginger, and shallots until minced. Add soy sauce and maple syrup; pulse to combine. Slowly add oil, and process until emulsified. Add sesame seeds, and pulse once.

Transfer marinade mixture to a shallow glass baking dish or a zip-top plastic bag. Add steak, and allow to marinate at least 30 minutes or up to 2 hours.

Heat grill or broiler to medium high. Grill or broil, 3 to 6 minutes on each side, or until tender and internal temperature reaches 135°. Let steak rest 10 minutes; slice thinly against the grain before serving.

Maple Barbecue Ribs and Sauce

• •

Ever since I learned this technique while working at Kraft, the recipe has been a family favorite.
It never fails to make fall-off-the-bone ribs, and it's easy to remember to cook them for 2½ hours at 250°.
Maple flavor from the sugar and syrup gives this recipe just enough sweetness.
Ribs can be made ahead of time and reheated right before serving.*

• •

makes 4–6 servings

RIBS
¼ cup maple sugar
3 tablespoons kosher salt
3 tablespoons smoked paprika
1½ tablespoons garlic powder
1½ tablespoons onion powder
1½ tablespoons black pepper
2 full racks baby back ribs
½ cup water

SAUCE
1 (6-ounce) can tomato paste
⅓ cup maple syrup with
   chili powder
¼ cup apple cider vinegar
¼ cup ketchup
2 tablespoons spicy
   brown mustard
1 tablespoon soy sauce
1 tablespoon
   Worcestershire sauce
1 teaspoon garlic powder
1 teaspoon onion powder
1 teaspoon chili powder
1 teaspoon smoked paprika

Preheat oven to 250°.

To make ribs, combine maple sugar and next 5 ingredients in a small bowl. Cover both sides of ribs with dry rub mixture. Pour ½ cup water in bottom of a large roasting pan with rack. Stand ribs up on edge or bone side down on rack so fat drains away.

Roast ribs, covered, 2½ hours or until tender and falling off the bone.

To make sauce, whisk tomato paste and next 10 ingredients in a saucepan over medium-low heat until combined. Simmer until flavors have melded. Taste and season.

Cut ribs apart and serve with sauce.

*To reheat, cut racks of ribs into 2 pieces and grill over medium heat 2 to 3 minutes on each side. Brush with sauce; cover and let sauce bake on. Cut ribs apart and serve with remaining sauce on the side.

Maple-Basted Roasted Turkey Breast

This is really good when you are hungry for roast turkey but don't want to make a whole bird. I serve this with Company's Coming Salad (page 78) and Maple-Bacon Brussels Sprouts (page 70) for a delicious maple-flavored meal.

makes 6–8 servings

TURKEY
1 cup water or apple juice
1 (7- to 8-pound) whole bone-in
    turkey breast*
Salt, to taste
½ apple, cut in half
½ onion, peeled and quartered
1 stalk celery, halved
1 sprig fresh rosemary
1 sprig fresh thyme

GLAZE
½ cup butter
½ cup maple syrup

Preheat oven to 350°. Line a shallow roasting pan with aluminum foil. Pour 1 cup water or apple juice in bottom of pan.

To make turkey breast, rinse with cold water; pat dry and sprinkle cavity with salt. Place turkey upright in pan, and stuff cavity with apple, onion, celery, rosemary, and thyme.

To make glaze, melt butter with maple syrup in a small saucepan over low heat. Pour over turkey to coat.

Roast turkey 2-2½ hours, basting with pan juices as desired, until an instant-read thermometer registers 175–180°.

Let turkey rest 20 minutes before slicing. Heat pan juices and pour over sliced meat. Serve hot.

*This recipe can be used for a whole turkey as well; increase ingredients as needed.

sides

Maple-Bacon Brussels Sprouts

This recipe will turn any brussels sprouts hater into a brussels sprouts lover.
Be careful not to burn them.

makes 4–6 servings

INGREDIENTS
1-1¼ pounds brussels sprouts, stemmed and cut in half lengthwise or sliced thin
4 slices bacon, cut into ½-inch pieces
2 tablespoons olive oil
2 tablespoons maple syrup
Salt and pepper, to taste

Preheat oven to 400°.

Place brussels sprouts in a shallow roasting pan; top evenly with bacon pieces. Drizzle with olive oil and maple syrup, and stir to coat. Sprinkle with salt and pepper.

Roast 20 minutes or until sprouts are cooked and caramelized, stirring after 10 minutes.

Maple-Roasted Root Vegetables

Oven-roasting brings out the best in these vegetables, while maple syrup adds just the right amount of sweetness.

makes 6 servings

INGREDIENTS
3 medium-size carrots, peeled, halved, and cut into 3- to 4-inch pieces
3 medium-size parsnips, peeled, halved, and cut in to 3- to 4-inch pieces
1 turnip, peeled, halved, and cut into slivers
½ cup maple syrup
4 tablespoons butter
¼ cup bourbon or rum
1½ teaspoons salt
Freshly ground black pepper

Preheat oven 350°.

Arrange carrots, parsnips, and turnip in a shallow roasting pan.

Heat maple syrup and butter in a small saucepan over medium-low heat until butter is melted; remove from heat, and stir in bourbon. Pour syrup mixture over vegetables and stir to coat. Sprinkle with salt and pepper.

Bake, covered with aluminum foil, 25 minutes. Uncover; stir and bake 25 additional minutes or until tender.

Best Mashed Sweet Potatoes

Put away your recipe for sweet potatoes with melted marshmallows.
This rich recipe is full of natural sweet potato goodness.
I serve these at Thanksgiving and everyone gobbles them up.
Even better, this recipe may be made ahead and stored in the refrigerator up to 5 days.

makes 8–10 servings

INGREDIENTS
4–6 large sweet potatoes
8 sprigs thyme, divided
6 tablespoons butter
¼ cup maple syrup
Salt and freshly ground
   black pepper

Preheat oven to 300°.

On a large sheet of heavy-duty aluminum foil, place 2 to 3 potatoes and 3 sprigs thyme. Fold foil around potatoes and seal tightly. Repeat with remaining 2 to 3 potatoes and 3 sprigs thyme. Place pouches on a baking pan, and roast 2 hours. Remove from oven; cool.

Meanwhile, melt butter in a small saucepan over medium-low heat until slightly browned. In the bowl of a stand-up electric mixer fitted with a whisk, add butter, maple syrup, and thyme leaves from remaining 2 sprigs.

Peel sweet potatoes. Discard peelings and add potatoes to bowl of stand-up mixer; beat until mixture is smooth and fluffy. Season to taste with salt and pepper.

Maple Baked Beans

This recipe is a classic from my childhood. I like it so much that it's referred to as "Corrine's Beans" in my family. Serve this as a side dish for a picnic, tailgate, or a potluck.

makes 6 servings

INGREDIENTS

6 bacon strips, cut into
    1-inch pieces
1 pound lean ground beef
2 envelopes onion soup mix*
2 (28-ounce) cans baked
    beans, drained
¾ cup maple syrup
½ cup ketchup
2 tablespoons Dijon mustard
2 teaspoons cider vinegar

Cook bacon in a large skillet over medium heat until crispy. Remove and drain on paper towels, reserving drippings in skillet. Crumble and set aside.

Cook ground beef in drippings in skillet over medium-high heat until meat is browned and no longer pink; drain and return to skillet. Stir in soup mix, baked beans, maple syrup, ketchup, mustard, and vinegar to combine.

Preheat oven to 325°.

Transfer beef mixture to an oven-safe bean pot or Dutch oven; bake 1 hour. Sprinkle with crumbled bacon before serving.

*I prefer Lipton brand.

Company's Coming Salad

There's nothing like a nice homemade salad dressing—it's so much better than bottled.
Any combination of greens, fresh fruit, dried fruit, cheese, and candied nuts is welcome in this salad.

makes 1½ cups dressing

DRESSING
¼ cup maple syrup
2 tablespoons lemon juice
1 tablespoon Dijon mustard
1 cup extra virgin olive oil
¼ teaspoon salt
⅛ teaspoon freshly ground
   black pepper

SALAD
16 cups mixed greens

TOPPINGS
1 large pear, thinly sliced; 1 cup
   sweetened dried cranberries;
   1 cup Maple-Glazed Nuts (see
   page 106); 1 (4-ounce) package goat cheese, crumbled

To make dressing, process maple syrup, lemon juice, and mustard in the bowl of a food processor with a metal blade until combined. With machine running, slowly add olive oil, and process until emulsified. Season with salt and pepper; process and taste, adding more, if necessary.

To make salad, toss mixed greens with desired toppings in a large bowl; serve with dressing.

sweets and desserts

Maple Nut Lace Cookies

· ·

These thin, toffee-like, maple-nut cookies are easy to make and fun to eat.
Make this recipe with purchased chopped pecans to ensure uniformity of size and smoothness of edges.

· ·

makes about 16 cookies

INGREDIENTS
½ stick (4 tablespoons)
   unsalted butter
¼ cup sugar
3 tablespoons maple syrup
1 tablespoon light corn syrup
1 teaspoon maple extract
½ cup chopped pecans
3 tablespoons all-purpose flour

Preheat oven to 325°. Line a baking sheet with parchment paper.

In a small saucepan over low heat, melt butter; stir in sugar, maple syrup, and corn syrup until combined. Stir in maple extract, pecans, and flour until combined. Cook, stirring gently, 1 minute.

Drop dough by tablespoons, 3 inches apart, onto prepared pan; bake 11 minutes. The cookies spread, so, after 5 minutes, push edges in with a spatula to keep cookies about 3 inches across. Cool on pan 3 to 4 minutes; transfer to a wire rack to cool completely.

Maple Leaf Cutout Cookies

· ·

This dough's consistency is great for making cutout cookies. Do not skip the chilling step.

· ·

makes 20 cookies

INGREDIENTS

¾ cup unsalted butter
¼ cup granulated sugar
1 teaspoon maple extract
2 tablespoons maple syrup
1½ cups all-purpose flour
1 teaspoon baking powder
¼ teaspoon salt
½ cup maple sugar

In the bowl of a stand-up electric mixer, beat butter and granulated sugar until light and fluffy. Beat in maple extract and syrup until combined.

In a large bowl, sift together flour, baking powder, and salt; add to butter mixture, mixing until incorporated.

Roll dough to ¼-inch thickness between two sheets of parchment paper. Lift and place on a cookie sheet, and chill 1 to 2 hours.

Preheat oven to 300°.

Peel off top sheet of parchment paper. Cut dough (on parchment paper on pan) with a maple leaf-shaped cutter. Remove excess dough, leaving cookies on pan, and sprinkle with maple sugar. (Reroll dough scraps and make more cookies.)

Bake 12 to 14 minutes or until edges are lightly golden. Transfer to a wire rack to cool completely. Store in an airtight container.

Spicy Maple Syrup Cookies

This recipe was inspired by *The Pioneer Woman's* Spicy Molasses Cookies.

makes 45 cookies

INGREDIENTS
1 cup light brown sugar
½ cup butter-flavored shortening
¼ cup unsalted butter, softened
¼ cup maple syrup
1 egg
2 cups all-purpose flour
2½ teaspoons baking soda
1 teaspoon cinnamon
1 teaspoon ginger
½ teaspoon ground cloves
¼ teaspoon ground cardamom
¼ teaspoon salt
¼ cup granulated sugar
Maple sugar

Preheat oven to 350°.

In the bowl of a stand-up electric mixer, beat brown sugar, shortening, butter, and maple syrup; add egg, and mix until well combined.

Combine flour and next 6 ingredients in a large bowl. Gradually add flour mixture to brown sugar mixture, beating lightly to combine.

Place granulated sugar in a small bowl. Measure out dough with a small scoop, shape into balls, and roll in granulated sugar. Place balls on baking sheets; flatten slightly, and sprinkle lightly with maple sugar. Bake 9 to 11 minutes. (Allow cookies to bake for about 1 minute after cracks begin to appear.)

Maple Fruit Crisp

Most of the sweetness here comes naturally from the fruit and maple syrup.
Use any fruit you have on hand, whether it's fresh or frozen.

makes 6–8 servings

TOPPING
½ cup rolled oats
¼ cup chopped walnuts
  or almonds
¼ cup whole-wheat pastry flour
¼ cup sugar
¼ teaspoon salt
¼ cup butter, cut into pieces
3–4 tablespoons maple syrup

FILLING
1 cup chopped frozen peaches
  or 2 fresh peaches, peeled,
  pitted, and chopped
2 cups mixed blueberries, rasp-
  berries, and blackberries
¼ cup dried cranberries
½ teaspoon ground cinnamon
½ teaspoon ginger
1 tablespoon all-purpose flour
4–5 tablespoons maple syrup

Preheat oven to 350°.

To make topping, toast oats and nuts on a rimmed baking sheet in the oven 10 to 12 minutes, stirring halfway through, until golden brown and fragrant. Allow to cool.

In the bowl of a food processor with a metal blade, pulse flour, sugar, and salt 2 to 3 times. Sprinkle butter over flour mixture, and pulse until mixture resembles coarse meal. Stir in toasted oats mixture, and drizzle with 3 to 4 tablespoons maple syrup. Process topping mixture until it clumps.

To make filling, stir together peaches and next 2 ingredients in a large bowl. In a small bowl, stir together cinnamon, ginger, and flour to combine. Drizzle with 4 to 5 tablespoons maple syrup to taste.

Spread filling mixture into an 8-inch square baking dish. Sprinkle with topping mixture and bake 30 to 40 minutes or until fruit is bubbling and topping is crisp.

Maple Brownies
with Maple Frosting

These dark chocolate—but not bitter—brownies are my new favorite.
They have a fudge-cake consistency, they cut nicely, and are good frosted or plain.

makes 25–30 brownies

BROWNIES

1 cup unsalted butter
1 (12-ounce) package semisweet
   chocolate chips
3 ounces milk chocolate
3 large eggs
1½ tablespoons cacao nibs,
   chopped into small pieces
1 tablespoon maple extract
1 cup granulated sugar
⅛ cup maple sugar
¾ cup all-purpose flour
1½ teaspoons baking powder
½ teaspoon salt

FROSTING

7 tablespoons butter, softened
   and at room temperature
½ cup muscovado or dark
   brown sugar
6 tablespoons maple syrup
1 (8-ounce) package cream
   cheese, softened and at
   room temperature

Preheat oven to 350°. Lightly grease a 9x9-inch baking pan or line with aluminum foil.

To make brownies, melt 1 cup butter, chocolate, and milk chocolate together in a medium-size glass or metal bowl over a saucepan of simmering water, stirring constantly. Remove from heat to cool.

In a large mixing bowl, stir together eggs, nibs, maple extract, granulated sugar, and maple sugar. Stir in cooled chocolate mixture.

Sift together flour, baking powder, and salt in a small bowl. Stir flour mixture into chocolate mixture. Pour batter into prepared pan.

Bake 20 minutes; turn pan, and bake 15 more minutes or until center is set and edges begin to pull away from sides of pan. Cool.

To make frosting, beat together 7 tablespoons butter, muscovado sugar, and maple syrup until light and airy. Add cream cheese; beat until smooth. Frost brownies, if desired. Store, covered, in the refrigerator. Cut into squares before serving.

Maple Fudge

· ·

This is an indulgent sweet staple that makes a fabulous gift. It lasts for a long time in an airtight container. Like all candy, it is a bit tricky to make. Gather all of your equipment, including a candy thermometer, before you begin, as this recipe requires all of your attention.

· ·

makes 32–36 pieces

INGREDIENTS
2 cups maple syrup
2 tablespoons light corn syrup
1 cup heavy cream
3 tablespoons butter, cut
   into pieces
½ cup chopped walnuts

Line a 9x5-inch pan with aluminum foil; lightly grease with cooking spray or coat with butter.*

In a heavy 4-quart saucepan, stir together maple syrup and corn syrup. Attach a candy thermometer to side of pan, and bring syrup mixture to a boil over medium heat. Reduce heat and simmer 5 minutes.

Pour in heavy cream (do not stir). Continue cooking about 20 minutes or until temperature reaches 235° (soft ball stage). If crystals start to form along the edge, dip a pastry brush in water and wash the sides of the pan.

Remove from heat, and add butter (do not stir). Allow mixture to cool in pan 8 minutes. Remove candy thermometer. Using an electric hand mixer, beat mixture in pan at medium speed 3 to 5 minutes or until mixture thickens, lightens in color, and loses its sheen yet remains creamy and pourable.

Quickly spread fudge mixture into prepared pan, smoothing with a spatula. Sprinkle with walnuts, pressing lightly. Refrigerate 2 to 3 hours. Lift fudge from pan and cut into 1-inch squares.

*A 9x6 aluminum foil fudge pan may be substituted.

Maple Mousse

· ·

This old-fashioned dessert has a lovely pudding-like texture. Because it contains uncooked egg whites, I recommend using pasteurized eggs when preparing this recipe.

· ·

makes 5 servings

INGREDIENTS

1 teaspoon unflavored gelatin mix
2 tablespoons water
2 pasteurized eggs, separated and divided
2 tablespoons brown sugar
¾ cup maple syrup
¾ cup heavy whipping cream
Maple Leaf Cutout Cookies (page 84) or purchased maple leaf-shaped cookies

Sprinkle gelatin mix over 2 tablespoons water in a glass measuring cup; let sit 3 to 5 minutes or until gelatin reaches an applesauce consistency. Microwave 20 seconds and stir to dissolve.

Beat egg yolks (reserving egg whites) and brown sugar together in a medium-size metal bowl. Stir in maple syrup. Place bowl over a saucepan of simmering water and cook, whisking constantly, about 15 minutes or until custard mixture thickens.

Remove custard from heat. Stir in liquid gelatin. Cool; cover with plastic wrap and refrigerate 30 minutes.

Whip egg whites in a small bowl until firm. In a separate bowl, whip cream until firm. Fold both alternately into custard. Transfer to 5 dessert glasses. Chill 4 hours before serving with cookies.

Carrot Cake with Maple Syrup Frosting

Carrot cake is my favorite and the only type of cake I crave.
I always bake it for my husband's birthday. The cream cheese frosting is the perfect touch.

makes 1 (2-layer) cake

CAKE
2½ cups all-purpose flour
1 teaspoon baking soda
1 teaspoon cinnamon
½ teaspoon salt
½ cup coconut oil
¾ cup maple syrup
1 teaspoon vanilla or
    maple extract
3 eggs
1 cup finely grated carrots
1 cup crushed pineapple,
    drained
1 cup shredded coconut
1 cup chopped walnuts

FROSTING
2 (8-ounce) packages cream
    cheese, softened and at
    room temperature
½ cup butter, softened and at
    room temperature
¼ cup maple syrup
2 cups powdered sugar (sifted)

Preheat oven to 350°. Lightly grease 2 (8- or 9-inch) round cake pans with nonstick baking spray. Line with a parchment paper round.

To make cake, whisk together flour, baking soda, cinnamon, and salt in a large bowl.

In the bowl of a stand-up electric mixer, combine oil, ¾ cup maple syrup, and extract; add eggs, one at a time. Add flour mixture and stir until blended. Stir in carrots, pineapple, coconut, and nuts by hand.

Divide batter between prepared pans. Bake 40 minutes or until a toothpick inserted in center comes out clean. Cool cakes completely before frosting.

To make frosting, combine cream cheese and butter in the bowl of a stand-up electric mixer. Whisk in ¼ cup maple syrup and powdered sugar until frosting is fluffy. Refrigerate 10 to 20 minutes. Frost cake before serving.

Maple Pecan Pie

Pecan pie is a Thanksgiving staple. Adding maple syrup makes it even more special.

makes 1 (9-inch) pie

INGREDIENTS
1 purchased refrigerated piecrust
⅓ cup butter
½ cup sugar
½ teaspoon salt
3 eggs
1 cup maple syrup
1 teaspoon vanilla extract
1⅔ cups whole pecans
Sweetened whipped cream
    (purchased or freshly whipped)

Preheat oven and bake piecrust according to package directions until lightly browned. Reduce oven temperature to 250°.

Melt butter in a medium-size glass or metal bowl over a saucepan of simmering water (see instructions for a double boiler, page 25). Remove bowl from heat. Stir in sugar and salt until moistened. Add eggs, one at a time, whisking to combine. Whisk in syrup and vanilla until mixture is smooth. Return bowl to heat, stirring until a candy thermometer registers 130°. Remove from heat and stir in pecans. Pour mixture into prepared crust. Bake 1 hour or until filling sets. Serve with whipped cream.

appetizers and beverages

Cowboy Caviar

This healthy, popular dip is a great answer to the question, "What can I bring to the party?"
Don't forget to pick up your favorite scoop-style chips.

makes 8 cups

BLACK-EYED PEA CAVIAR
2 (14-ounce) cans black-eyed
  peas, rinsed and drained
1 (14-ounce) can black beans,
  rinsed and drained
1½ cups fresh corn kernels
1½ cups chopped tomatoes
1 small red bell pepper, chopped
1 small yellow bell pepper,
  chopped
1 small orange bell pepper,
  chopped
¾ cup red onion, chopped
½ cup cilantro, chopped
1 jalapeño, seeded and
  finely chopped

DRESSING
3 tablespoons white wine vinegar
2 cloves garlic, peeled
1 tablespoon Italian seasoning
1 tablespoon maple syrup
1½ teaspoons salt
⅛ teaspoon red pepper flakes
Freshly ground black pepper,
  to taste
⅓ cup olive oil
1 ripe avocado, cubed
Scoop-style corn chips

To make "caviar," combine black-eyed peas and next
9 ingredients in a large bowl.

To make dressing, process vinegar, garlic, Italian seasoning,
maple syrup, salt, red pepper flakes, and black pepper in
the bowl of a food processor with a metal blade until garlic
is finely minced. Slowly add olive oil until dressing mixture
is emulsified.

Drizzle dressing over black-eyed pea mixture, and toss to
combine. Allow to sit 20 minutes. Meanwhile, peel, seed,
and cube avocado. Gently fold in avocado just before serving
with scoop-style chips.

Maple Popcorn Party Mix

· ·

This is the perfect snack to munch on during major sporting events like the Super Bowl and the World Series. It has a little kick to it that will keep guests coming back for more.

· ·

makes 12–13 cups

INGREDIENTS
10 cups popped popcorn
1 cup salted mini pretzels
1 cup whole cashews
1 cup dry-roasted salted peanuts
¼ cup butter
¾ cup brown sugar
¼ cup maple syrup
1 tablespoon Sriracha sauce
1 teaspoon salt
1 tablespoon maple extract

Preheat oven to 300°. Line 2 baking sheets with aluminum foil.

Toss together popcorn, pretzels, and nuts in a large bowl.

Melt butter in a large saucepan over medium heat; stir in brown sugar, syrup, Sriracha, and salt. Bring to a boil, swirling pan to combine. When sugar is dissolved, boil for 2 minutes or until a candy thermometer registers 230°. Remove from heat and stir in maple extract.

Drizzle hot caramel mixture over popcorn mixture; toss to coat. Spread evenly on prepared baking sheets. Bake 20 minutes or until caramel has set, stirring occasionally. Cool on pans. Transfer to a large serving bowl.

Maple-Glazed Nuts

These nuts are great in a salad or as an accompaniment to a cheese plate.
Try them alongside an aged cheddar or a sheep's milk cheese.

makes 2 cups

INGREDIENTS
⅓ cup maple syrup
2 cups whole walnut halves
½ teaspoon salt
1 teaspoon maple sugar

Heat a dry skillet over medium-high heat. Add maple syrup and walnuts, gently folding and stirring to coat, about 3 minutes or until caramelized. While nuts are hot and a bit sticky, sprinkle with salt and maple sugar. Dump out onto aluminum foil; let cool and harden. Break and peel nuts off foil.

Maple-Bacon Popcorn

The combination of the sweet maple, salty popcorn, and smoky bacon flavors makes for a great snack.

makes 10 cups

INGREDIENTS
10 cups popped popcorn, salted
1 pound bacon, cut into
    1-inch pieces
½ cup maple syrup
Salt and freshly ground black
    pepper, to taste

Preheat oven to 350°. Line a rimmed baking sheet with aluminum foil; spread out popcorn evenly on sheet.

Cook bacon in a skillet over medium heat until crispy. Remove and drain on paper towels, reserving 2 tablespoons drippings in pan. Stir in maple syrup. Drizzle syrup mixture over popcorn on prepared pan. Crumble bacon on top. Stir to coat and spread out evenly on pan. Season liberally with salt and pepper. Bake 10 to 14 minutes.

Bloody Mary

I love to go all in with my Bloody Mary garnishes—the more, the merrier.
This is an additional use for the Maple Syrup-Glazed Bacon (page 36).

makes 1 serving

INGREDIENTS
Lime juice
Maple sugar
Ice
Lime or lemon wedge
2 ounces vodka
7 ounces Spicy Bloody Mary Mix
Garnishes: Skewered Maple
    Syrup-Glazed Bacon (page
    36), summer sausage, cooked
    shrimp, cheese cubes, celery,
    dill pickle spears, olives, and
    lemon wedges

Pour lime juice and maple sugar into separate saucers. Dip 1 (16-ounce) glass first in lime juice and then in maple sugar to coat edge. Fill glass with ice. Squeeze lime wedge into glass, and add vodka. Top with Bloody Mary mix; stir to combine. Garnish, if desired.

Maple Chai Tea

Chai is a soothing hot drink. The maple syrup gives it a sweet earthiness.

makes 1 serving

INGREDIENTS

½ cup milk or almond milk
1 tablespoon maple syrup
¼ teaspoon maple extract
1 cup hot green tea (prepared in
   a plunge pot for best results)
Dash of cinnamon

In a small saucepan over low heat, stir together milk, maple syrup, and maple extract. Stir hot tea into milk mixture, and then pour into a mug. Sprinkle cinnamon on top before serving.

Maple Leaf Cocktail

Maple syrup and bourbon make for a great combination that's not too sweet and naturally good.

makes 1 serving

INGREDIENTS
Ice
2 tablespoons maple syrup
1 part bourbon
3 parts seltzer
Peel of 1 orange
Black cherries

Fill a highball glass with ice. Pour maple syrup over ice. Add bourbon and seltzer, stirring to combine. Add orange peel and desired amount of cherries.

Index